leap THROUGH TIME

City

First published in 2002 by Orpheus Books Ltd, 2 Church Green,
Witney, Oxon OX28 4AW

Created and produced by Nicholas Harris and Claire Aston,
Orpheus Books Ltd

Text Nicholas Harris

Illustrator Peter Dennis (*Linda Rogers Associates*)

Consultant Alex Werner, Museum of London

ISBN 1 901323 45 5

Printed and bound in Malaysia

leap THROUGH TIME

The Story of a

City

illustrated by

Peter Dennis

orpheus

Contents

4

Introduction

Imagine you are standing on a riverbank somewhere in Europe thousands of years ago. Some farmers make a small settlement there, taking advantage of the fertile land and plentiful supply of fish in the river. Over the centuries, others find the site favourable too. It is a good place to build a bridge and a port. Soon a town grows up, eventually becoming a bustling city.

The story told in this book is like a journey. It is not a journey you can make by plane, car or ship. In fact, you don't have to go anywhere at all. You are about to travel through *time*. With each turn of the page, the date moves forward a few hours, years or even centuries. Each new date—each stop on your journey—is like a chapter in the life of the city. The early days as a small farming settlement by the banks of the river, the Roman town, the medieval walled city with its cathedral and castle, the day, years later, when a great fire nearly destroyed it all, the rebuilding, the dark days of World War II bombing, the modern buildings of today—all tell the story of the city.

Look out for the baker. He appears in all of the illustrations. You should be able to identify him from his bright red hair!

Use this thumb index to travel through time! Just find the page you want to see and flip it open. This way you can make a quick comparison between one scene and another, even though some show events that took place many years apart. A little black arrow on the page points to the time of the scene illustrated on that page.

About 3000 years ago ...

A group of farming people have decided to build a settlement on the banks of a river. They have found a place where the ground is firm and dry, a little higher than marshland further upstream. All their needs are close by. Trees in the surrounding forest are cut down for firewood and for building huts and fences. Flat, fertile land where the trees have already been cleared is good for growing crops and grazing livestock. The settlers hunt animals in the forest, or catch fish and birds. The river is also a useful way of travelling further afield.

Stone circle

Ramparts

Ditch

Boat-building

Spinning cloth

Weaving

Firewood

Pottery kiln

Baking bread

Pot-making

Making flour

The settlers work hard. Nearly everything they need they must find or make for themselves. There are no shops, so everyone who is able helps make clothes, pots, boats and weapons. They use bronze, a mixture of copper and tin, to make tools, although wood and stone are still widely used.

The people make offerings to their ancestors, believing that, in return, their harvest will be good, spring will return after winter and that disasters will not befall them.

Today their chief greets people from across the river, who arrive to trade their cloth for grain grown by the settlers.

Raised walkway

Drying fish

Trading vessel

Chief

Fishing boats

More than 1000 years later ...

The Romans have arrived. The remains of the farming village are now buried beneath the paved streets and stone buildings of a busy, prosperous town.

As the Roman armies swept across the country, they built fortresses. Here they found the best place to build a bridge across the river. The fortress was built to defend the river crossing. Soon a town grew up around it as shopkeepers, craftsmen and merchants arrived to sell their wares to the soldiers.

Fortress

Temple

Forum

Market

Baths

Butcher

Bakery

Tavern

Stepping stones

With its riverside port, the town has grown prosperous from trade. Today, however, a ship arriving at the quayside will load up not with goods but people—slaves for sale. A plot has been hatched by local tribesmen to free them. While some men pretend to scale the walls, a rescue party lies in wait . . .

THE ROMAN WAY OF LIFE

A people from central Italy, the Romans had, by about AD 120, built up a mighty empire across most of Europe. Their highly trained army crushed all opposition. Wherever the Romans went they brought their way of life with them. Skilful engineers and builders, they constructed bridges, roads, walls and buildings, some of which still survive today. Roman cities had centrally heated houses, public baths with hot water, theatres and temples. Their language, Latin, was spoken by everyone in the Roman Empire.

Amphitheatre

Warehouse

Bridge

Slaves

Rescuers

Soldiers

Look-out tower

The Romans have left their town. For a while, people carried on living in it even after the soldiers had abandoned the fortress. But with no trade, people fell on hard times. One by one they also left and their houses started to crumble.

the old town. Many of the Roman buildings, solidly made of stone, remain standing. But the new settlers, a farming people accustomed to building their houses only out of wood with straw thatch roofs, allow them to fall into ruin.

Roman fortress

Assembly hall

Cross

Milking

Blacksmith

Bakehouse

Weavin

Roman wall

10

It is a blustery autumn day in the village. Today's market, held in the square near the newly-erected cross, has suffered from the rainy conditions. The baker, blacksmith and other village craftsmen are hard at work indoors. The village thane (chief) watches men attempting to launch their boats.

BARBARIAN EUROPE

After many years under Roman rule, Europe in the 400s fell into turmoil. The Romans described the peoples who lived outside their empire as "barbarians", from the Latin word meaning "strange ones". Barbarian tribes, including the Huns, Goths, Vandals and Visigoths, swept westwards, attacking Rome and invading their lands. As the Roman Empire collapsed, new kingdoms emerged. The Franks ruled over France and Germany. Jutes, Angles and Saxons overran Britain.

Roman ruins

Thane

Monks

Antler-working

About 250 years later ...

The land now belongs to the Vikings, a people from Scandinavia. Finding this riverside village perfectly positioned as an inland port for their trading ships, they have built a new town where the old farming village once stood.

Like the people before them, the Vikings built their houses not from stone, but wood. Their town is made up of neat rows of cottages with thatched roofs and walls built of wattle and daub (woven branches plastered with mud). Only the stone Roman fortress and the town walls survive.

Roman fort

Cross

Bakery

Smith

Leather-workers

Well

Splitting wood

Roman wall

Besides houses and shops, the Viking town is full of workshops where potters, leatherworkers, silk-makers, carpenters metalworkers and boat-builders busy themselves. Ships, wide-bodied versions of the famous Viking longships, set sail for distant lands laden with goods to trade for silk, gold, silver, wine and dyes.

THE VIKINGS

The Vikings were a seafaring people from the Scandinavian countries of northern Europe. Between about 750 and 1100, they raided and looted many parts of Europe. They also settled in a number of lands, including England, France, Russia, Iceland and Greenland. Travelling in their sturdy, ocean-going wooden ships, Viking explorers even sailed as far afield as North America. Warriors, traders, craftsmen and farmers, the Vikings were a dominant force in Northern Europe for more than three centuries.

Assembly hall

Warship

Boat-builders

Silks

Trading vessel

About 400 years later ...

The town has become larger and busier. Its favourable position as both a port and a river crossing (there is once more a bridge over the river, now built of stone), has attracted more people to live and work there. The small wattle and daub cottages of Viking times have been replaced by larger and sturdier timber-framed houses, most with two floors rather than just one.

Cathedral

Castle

Thatcher

Bakery

Beggars

Blacksmith's forge

Market

Stone from the ruined Roman fortress has been used to build a magnificent new castle, home of the local lord, while the old Roman walls have been rebuilt to provide extra defences for the town. Towering above the tightly packed townspeople's homes is a huge, new, stone-built cathedral.

Today is market day and people come to town to buy and sell their wares. It is also a good opportunity for entertainers, beggars and thieves to take money from passers-by! The air is filled both with the smells of food and animals, and the cries of traders and shopkeepers announcing what they have for sale.

Windmill

City walls

Bridge

Fish market

Merchant's house

Inn

Kitchen

Buttery

Thieves

15

Nearly 400 years later ...

Darkness falls one warm summer's evening in the mid-1600s. Since our last visit to the city, the population has grown once more. A number of people have become wealthier and now live in grander, more comfortable houses.

Cathedral

Castle

Robber

Bakehouse

Apothecary

Plague doctor

w into
hey
es not only
business
t, culture
—just as
. Although
althy and
city was
for
e and
ments.

But, despite the city's prosperity, disease and vermin are still rife. Tonight, the plague doctor is going on his rounds, and it has been a busy day at the apothecary's (chemists).

Crime is another part of city life. A gang of smugglers down at the quayside is about to be surprised by soldiers. Robbers lurk in dark alleys and fights are breaking out at the inn.

Meanwhile, the baker retires to bed, unaware that a small fire has broken out in the bakehouse below . . .

1000 BC

AD 120

AD 620

AD 870

1270

1650

City walls

Theatre

Bridge

Soldiers

Inn

Smugglers

Sweep

17

Later that night ...

The city is an inferno! Fanned by an eager wind, the fire has quickly consumed the bakehouse and spread to other nearby buildings. With so much dry wood the whole of the city centre is soon alight.

Although many town dwellings were built of wood and crowded closely together in narrow streets, there was no fire service. This fire squirt *(above)* was the only means to fight fires. It was not until the 18th century that mechanical water pumps *(below)* were invented.

Castle

Cathedral

Fleeing the city

As flames claim their homes, the city's inhabitants gather up their possessions and flee in panic. At the quayside they crowd on to boats. The guards rescue the barrels of brandy hurriedly left behind by the smugglers.

Others stay and attempt to fight the fire. But there are neither water pumps nor hoses, only buckets or squirting devices. Some try to beat back the flames with brooms. Gunpowder is used to blow up buildings and create spaces between them to stop the fire spreading. Meanwhile, the baker looks on, aghast.

Making a fire-break

Escape by boat

Fire squirt

Beating the flames

1000 BC

AD 120

AD 620

AD 870

1270

1650

Later that night

19

The next morning ...

His wife tries to comfort him, but the baker is beside himself with misery. All around him, the city lies in ruins with only the brick chimneys standing among the charred timbers. Just the walls of a few brick or stone buildings, including the cathedral, have survived. The old bridge was saved from being burnt down by the fire-break.

Cathedral

Castle

Brick chimneys

European people lived in fear of the plague for hundreds of years. Carried by fleas that lived on black rats, plague swept the continent in the 14th century, reducing the population by a third in some countries. Because many townspeople lived in closely-packed houses, the disease could spread very easily. The destruction of old houses by fire and rebuilding the city with wider streets helped to wipe out the plague.

The rain, which eventually put out the fire, has stopped. Gradually, the people of the city return to the smouldering ruins of their old homes and wonder where they will live now.

GREAT FIRE OF LONDON

The Great Fire of London broke out on Sunday 2nd September 1666. While only eight or nine people died as a direct cause of the fire, seven-eighths of the city, including 13,000 houses and 87 churches, was destroyed. It started at a baker's shop in Pudding Lane and continued until firefighters finally succeeded in putting it out the following Friday. Many Londoners refused to allow their houses to be pulled down to create fire-breaks, making it easier for the fire to spread.

Bridge

Brick house still standing

1000 BC

AD 120

AD 620

AD 870

1270

1650

Later that night

The next morning

Manufacturing industries were set up in Europe in the 18th and 19th centuries. At the same time, the rich got richer and the poor became poorer. They all lived quite close together in cities. The well-to-do *(above)* wore fine clothes and mixed in fashionable society. Some of the very poor *(below)* turned to crime or excessive drinking.

About 120 years later ...

The city has been rebuilt and is, once again, a busy centre of commerce. The streets are wider and the houses are made of brick with tiled roofs. If a fire were to break out again, it is unlikely the whole city would burn down this time.

A number of people, such as lawyers, doctors, bankers and merchants, have well-paid jobs. They own grand town-houses, or live in spacious houses with gardens on the outskirts of the city.

Cathedral

Castle

Servant's bedroom

Baker

Fish barrow

Newspaper seller

Thatchers

Water pump

Soldiers

Laying pipes

The well-to-do take sedan chairs or carriages to travel through the dirty and often crowded streets. Other vehicles on the road are stagecoaches, which bring people from different parts of the country into the city (where they stay in coaching inns).

Thieves and pick-pockets roam the streets. The presence of nightwatchmen helps to reduce crime.

People come to the city to look for work. There are workshops, where cloth is made, and warehouses, where goods are stored. But press-gangs and soldiers are always on the look-out to force people to join the army or navy.

1000 BC

AD 120

AD 620

AD 870

1270

1650

Later that night

The next morning

1770

Bridge

Stagecoach

Coaching
inn

Quay-
side

Warehouse

Press-gang

23

By the late 19th century, all kinds of people lived in the city. Labourers and servants were the most numerous. Although some became better-off, many were still poor *(above)*. They lived in cramped, decaying houses, known as slums. Shop- and office-workers formed a lower middle class, while lawyers, doctors and factory owners made up an upper middle class *(below)*. People lived in different areas of the city according to their wealth.

A hundred years later ...

The industrial age has arrived. The city has expanded hugely as more and more people have come from the countryside to work in the factories. With the invention of the steam engine (which provides the power used by the factories' machines) has come the railway. An iron bridge and a brick viaduct carry steam trains into the heart of the city. Gas lighting and underground sewers make the streets safer and cleaner.

Toys

Department store

Hats

Clothes

Office

Chemist

Funeral

Chestnut seller

Postman

Drain

Milk seller

Roman wall

Sewer

Sweep

The old riverside warehouse is now a lodging house for people who have moved to the city. Poverty and over-crowding have become problems as too many people need to find somewhere to live in a city where there are too few houses.

Ships needed for trade with lands overseas are now too large to dock at the riverside. So the quayside is now used by barges, bringing goods from the seaports.

On this winter's day, the cobbled streets are full of traffic—horse-drawn carts and carriages. The baker, a street-seller, does brisk business in hot muffins.

Steam train

Viaduct

Railway bridge

Barge

Inn

Bus

Lodging house

25

The year 1940

War has broken out and the city is under attack from the air. As air-raid sirens shriek their warnings, people dash to find underground shelters. Soon planes appear in the skies overhead and drop bombs on the city. Powerful search beams flit across the night sky as soldiers manning anti-aircraft guns take aim at the enemy planes.

By the middle of the 20th century, many more people lived in cities than in the country. More and more people moved to larger houses further away from the city centre. From there they could travel into the city by train, tram or bus.

Many towns and cities in Europe were damaged or destroyed as a result of bombing by aircraft during World War II. Air-raid shelters were built to protect city-dwellers. In Britain, children were evacuated (sent away) to live in small towns or country areas away from the danger.

Department store

Spy

Looter

Home shelter

Firefighters

Water pump

Anti-aircraft gun

Underground shelter

Several bombs crash down. Some explode and destroy buildings. Others are fire-bombs, which cause a number of fires to break out. Firefighters rush to the scene with their hoses. Ambulances stand by to take injured people to hospital.

WORLD WAR TWO

Between 1939 and 1945, war was fought between the Axis powers—Germany, Italy and Japan—and the Allies—Britain, the Commonwealth countries, France, the Soviet Union and the USA. German forces quickly overran most of Europe, while Japan invaded countries of the Far East and the Pacific islands. Battles raged all over the world as the Allies fought back. In European cities, bombing raids destroyed buildings and killed many people.

Exploding bomb

Putting out fire bombs

Unexploded bombs

Ambulance

Bomber

Air-raid shelter

Escaping crew

1000 BC

AD 120

AD 620

AD 870

1270

1650

Later that night

The next morning

1770

1870

1940

27

Today

The city suffered great damage during the war, but afterwards many parts of it were rebuilt. Now there are many new buildings. Cars, and trams take people across the city, while some streets are reserved for pedestrians only. Speedboats and yachts are moored along the old quayside.

Crowded with shoppers and office-workers during the day, city streets are filled with people going to bars, restaurants, nightclubs, cinemas and theatres in the evening.

Cities are built up on top of the remains of old settlements. Above a modern underground railway tunnel (seen in this cross-section through the ground) are relics of thousands of years of history. They include a mammoth skeleton, the foundations of a Roman building and ashes from the Great Fire.

Clothes shop

Blimp (type of airship)

Castle

Cathedral

Shopping centre

Tram

Roman wall

Busker

"Vikings"

Archaeological dig

Of course, many old buildings dating from far back in the city's history still remain standing. They include the castle, the cathedral and a small house in the city centre that survived the Great Fire. It is now a museum.

Archaeologists are working on a site. They have dug down beneath the ground and discovered remains of the old Viking town. They can only imagine what it once was like. You can look back through this book to see the real thing!

Mosque

Office block

Warehouse converted to flats

Museum

Quayside

TV crew

Market

1000 BC

AD 120

AD 620

AD 870

1270

1650

Later that night

The next morning

1770

1870

1940

Today

Glossary

Apothecary A member of the medical profession who kept a shop for drugs and medicines.

Archaeologist A person who studies human life in the past, using the evidence from finds buried in the ground or under the sea.

Barge A flat-bottomed boat used for carrying goods on rivers or canals.

Blacksmith A person who makes or shapes iron objects, using heat to melt or soften the metal.

Cathedral A church which houses the bishop's seat (the *cathedra*). Bishops are important leaders of the Christian Church and cathedrals are the main churches in a Christian country.

City A large town. In some countries, a city is a town that has a cathedral, or one that has been given the official title of "city" by the government or monarch.

Commerce Trade (buying and selling of goods) between nations or individuals.

Culture The artistic life of a place and its people. An artist is someone who uses his or her skill to produce works of beauty or imagination.

Fire-break A strip of land or a group of buildings cleared to stop the spread of fire.

Fortress A place that has been fortified against attack, usually by building high or thick walls, ditches and other defences. (A fort is a small fortress)

Manufacturing industry The making of goods on a large scale using machines in factories.

Merchant Someone who makes a living out of buying and selling goods.

Muffin A soft cake, eaten hot with butter.

Nightwatchman A person who keeps watch over a town or city, rather like a policeman.

Plague A deadly disease spread by rat-fleas from rats to humans.

Press-gang A group of sailors who had the power to force men to join the navy. This practice died out in the 19th century.

Quayside A place for the loading and unloading of boats and ships.

Sedan chair A covered chair for a single person carried on two poles.

Sewer An underground channel or tunnel into which waste from house-drains and streets runs.

Stagecoach A passenger coach that runs regularly from one resting place on a journey to the next.

Vermin A general name for animals that are pests or cause disease. Rats and mice in places where people live are often described as vermin.

Warehouse A place where goods for sale are kept.

Wattle and daub A way of building in which wattle-work (woven branches) is plastered with mud.

Index